Daily Dose of Melancholy

Essee Jones

Essee Jones

DAILY DOSE OF
MELANCHOLY

For Pepaw, save me some.

Copyright © 2022 by Essee Jones

All rights reserved. No part of this book may be reproduced in any manner whatsoever without written permission except in the case of brief quotations embodied in critical articles and reviews.

First Printing, 2022

Forward

I hope these words destroy aloneness. Make seemingly unrelatable experiences relatable. Explore two conflicting ideas that can be equally true. And most of all, I hope they illuminate the beauty in the sadness, the possibilities in the breaking, and the fertility amongst the futile.

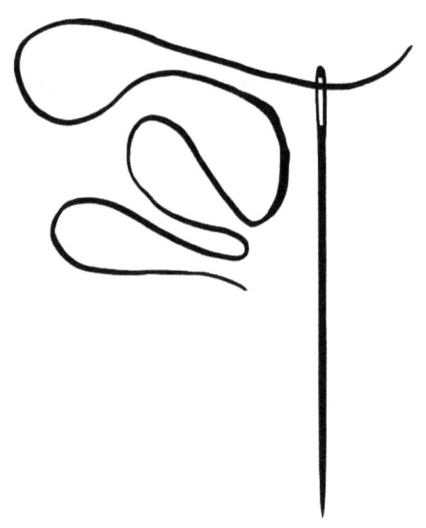

Depths

Have you ever watched people when they first get to the beach?

They take off running into the inviting water, abruptly stopping waist-high as if finally coming to their senses...hesitant of the deep and all it holds. The waves rocking back and forth, welcoming yet warning...pushing and pulling.

And I think of myself.

Of the ocean inside me, begging and inviting someone to come charging in with joy, yet hesitant and distant when I consider that means giving them access to the deepest parts of me...the treasures and dangers deep below the surface...pushing and pulling.

And maybe that's why I don't like wearing my glasses.

The fear of seeing people too closely and peering into their depths...afraid that means they can see into mine too. So I struggle and squint and strain only when I really want to pick up those details to see more...pushing and pulling.

Spinster

The cool night air reminded her of sneaking out as a teenager to meet her equally infatuated, yet equally misguided, adolescent love.

Those spring nights provided enough warmth to expose just enough skin to provoke the imagination, and cool enough to keep goosebumps just below the surface...to be drawn out by the gentlest of touches.

The still of those nights seemed to seal whispered promises and intimate kisses. Maybe it was the illusion that the rest of the world slept while they shared those precious moments that made forever seem possible, but enough sunrises later proved those early spring evenings were sweeter with the flavor of innocence and naivety.

Each spring brought more and more blossoms of desire for intimacy and belonging….as well as responsibilities.

With the wisdom of knowing the sun closely follows the moon, her youthful anticipation for spring evenings grew to be a heavy reminder of what she lacked and would probably never find again.

Committing to adult love was accepting to forever pay for the other's emotional debt accumulated over the years...an ever-growing sum.

The cool night air blew away her youthful reverie and prompted her to untie her jacket from around her waist and shrug it on to protect herself from the penetrating chill of loneliness.

Thrive

I wonder what it would be like to be held by the air…

Not weightless, that wouldn't be existing.

I want to exist, but just not as heavily as I have been.

I envy the birds in the sky, resting on a draft, flapping their wings only every so often.

Smooth, effortless, peaceful.

Thriving.

I pity the whales in the sea, created for oxygen but trapped in the water, coming up for air every half hour.

Loud, bulky, tired.

Surviving.

I feel as if I have been swimming for years.

Sleeping with one eye opening, traveling to the surface every half hour just to survive.

When will I find my wings?

Empty

I used to think love was like a boomerang; the harder I threw it out into the world, the more it would come back to me. But here I am empty handed and empty hearted.

Self-Harm

Hurt

The pulse quickened and breaths became shorter

Anger

The pulse beat around the temples and breaths became ragged

Failure and Rejection.

The pulse pounded in the chest and breaths became desperate

Failure Rejection Failure Rejection

The pulse reverberated, stuck at the wrists and breathing didn't matter

Only the hammering of the relentless pulse echoing the words slamming into the skull

Failure Rejection Failure Rejection Worthless Worthless Worthless

Wrists pounding

Words slamming

Worthless Worthless Worthless

Need to silence, locate sharpened edge

Wrists vibrating

Words- Cut. It. Out.

Silence.

Relief…

Pain

Shame

Conviction

An uneasy conscience is heavy, but a guilty heart weighs more.

Villain

Maybe Disney really did screw her over.

All of those princesses waiting to be rescued and knights in shining armor with forced chivalry…

She confused falling in love with a watered down version of stockholm syndrome.

Creating this narrative that her worthiness lied in being helpless.

And in truth, she wasn't helpless.

There was no tower, no dragon, no evil queen, no curse…nothing to be saved from.

So she became her own monster.

Something to be saved from.

Dementia

I sat and listened as my Papaw recounted his life in Mount Olive, Mississippi with his wife Loretta. Which is all fine and good except for the fact he lived in Indianola, Mississippi and his wife was Margaret.

Conversations like these became more frequent and I watched as his brain struggled to remember the paths his life wandered, a map of decisions unfolding before me.

It was almost as if his current reality reflected a life of choices and paths taken had Margaret not been in his life…as if she was the placeholder and bookmark of his pages.

In her absence, he slowly transitioned into a ghost, haunting the pages and paths of his life.

Searching.

I watched as 60 years' worth of life, love, and adventures unraveled and I believed that love is watching someone die.

Self-Worth

Whenever I think of describing myself, the phrase "too much" always comes to mind. I'd like to think it was a phrase planted in my brain by others...but it feels familiar...like a part of me has always been aware of my personal heaviness...so I would break myself into pieces.

Exposing only certain pieces of myself at the appropriate time and place...I thought I was saving others from being intimidated or overwhelmed, but it was at my own expense of belittling myself.

Boxes

People like to build walls.

To protect, to divide, to claim territory, to prevent, to contain....

We try to contain life within neat boxes. But it's a major disillusionment to think that life happens in neat boxes.

But I guess that's why the phrase "think outside the box" exists.

And I get it, life appears to be much more manageable in a box.

It creates a false sense of security and purpose as if we can arrive at a destination, to feel as if we have accomplished something.

Society pushes and encourages us to march alongside the border until we hit a wall, then turn 90 degrees and do it again.

Diploma, job, marriage, baby.

March, corner, repeat.

But what are we missing outside those borders?

What happens when we shatter the illusion of "arriving" at success?

Infidelity

I noticed today that you deleted our pictures from your page, as if you could erase what happened. Whether the images still exist or not, you lived that season. We lived that season. And I wonder if you'll be honest with yourself and others that the relationship ended as soon as you cheated. But I know you would rather scratch that blemish away instead of acknowledging you had one in the first place. You'll scratch and scratch, making it bleed and fester, over and over again in an attempt to expedite the healing process, refusing to admit you're prolonging the hurt. Denying any blame or imperfection. And I hate that I tried to carry that weight for you, offered bandaids to assuage your guilt. I'm left still carrying that burden, the consequences of your actions, left in the wake of your coldness, a casualty of infidelity.

Illness

I never really related to the term mental illness, it seemed too dramatic. I would claim depression and anxiety because those were so normalized and accepted, idolized even. But mentally ill? That just made everyone uncomfortable. Am I contagious? Is this chronic? Should I be hospitalized? No way, just a little seasonal depression mixed with some anxiety. It wasn't until I was hyperventilating in the baking aisle of the grocery store that I fully understood the extent of my illness. Crushed by the weight of sudden self-awareness, the knowledge of my deteriorating mental health rapidly unfolding before me as I struggled to stand upright and breathe normally as tears slid down my cheeks. People were starting to notice. I just needed to purchase my flour and leave, get home, and crawl into bed. But I couldn't move. Each step forward triggered more uneven breaths, as if the steps forward carried me into the harsh reality of living with mental illness, solidifying my fate. This must be what prey felt like as they were cornered by a relentless predator. At least they had the advantage of physically facing their adversary…how am I supposed to know whether to run, cower, or fight against something I can't even see or describe? I shut my eyes and gripped the handle of the buggy as I tried breathing in for four counts, holding for four, and releasing for four more counts. I think that's what you were supposed to do? Slowly, my breathing became regular, my thoughts more streamlined. I could feel my feet below me and took a couple steps forward, so far so good. I opened my eyes and reached for the bag of flour, tossed it in my cart, and headed to the register. The cashier smiled at me as she scanned my items and asked "How're the holidays treating you?" I just shrugged and said "Oh you know, time for seasonal baking and depression." She laughed as she handed me my change and wished me a Merry Christmas.

Attachment

If there was one developmental skill I would unlearn, it would be object permanence.

Knowing and believing in an object's existence, even if you can't see it.

You showed me just enough love to construct a clear mental image of it, and when you took it away I found myself still searching for it.

How cruel of you to play peek-a-boo with my heart.

Coping

It wasn't a drinking problem…

Definitely not an alcoholic.

Just not great at drinking in moderation.

Maybe it was social anxiety that caused the uptick in refills.

Or the lack of next-day hangovers….

Or maybe after spending so much time and energy attending to other people's needs, oblivion felt like a welcome relief with the hope someone else would be the caretaker for once.

Lonely

I've been struggling to turn loneliness into solitude.

I think it's because I am comfortable with loneliness, it makes sense to me.

I am sad because I am alone.

But solitude?

Being content while remaining alone?

The idea of solitude makes me uncomfortable.

I think the discomfort comes from being uncomfortable with myself.

Not trusting myself.

Not believing in myself.

Not knowing myself.

Not loving myself.

That is the struggle, to know or to even become someone I can be content being alone with.

That is the most uncomfortable of all.

So maybe I will settle for being lonely with any partner that comes along.

Remaining sad in our loneliness.

Until one or the other discovers themself.

Expiration

A glimmer of metallic silver and blue on the cabinet shelf caught her eye as she unpacked groceries. She let out a long sigh as she hauled out the 12-pack of disgusting IPAs her ex left at her house a few months prior. She stood there staring at the box for a while, contemplating. She wouldn't drink them, because she had a good taste in beer, and neither would any of her roommates. She sure wasn't going to return them to the owner. But she couldn't quite bring herself to pour them out either…it would just take up so much time and the smell would make her stomach churn. She laughed to herself, recognizing she had done this same routine every week: noticing the case, debating action steps, doing nothing, then hiding the case away just to repeat the process a week later.

Enough was enough.

She carried the case over to the sink and began pouring out each of the cans. As she watched the amber liquid swirl down the drain she thought about all of the promises and plans that never came to fruition in that relationship.

Can two: her canceled birthday dinner.

Can four: oh don't worry about it, she's just a friend.

Can seven: turning the light off and going to sleep as she cried into her pillow.

Can nine: excuses.

Can eleven: lies.

After emptying all of the cans, she turned to the cardboard box to break it down for recycling as she noticed the expiration date…turns out they expired two months ago.

Milestones

All the mundane little moments build up.

Little pebbles forming milestones.

Tying her own shoes or unbuckling her own seat belt…

The long, exhausting mile buildup of failure after failure until one day, just a simple click, just a hop over the stone and she's done it.

She won't need me to unbuckle her seatbelt or tie her shoes for her ever again.

Each milestone crossed takes her closer to independence and further away from needing me.

Absence

I watched as I sat in the sand just past the edge of the water, marking where each wave landed- some reaching only past my ankle, others coming to my knee.

With my feet stretched out before me, I noted the soft creases in the sand created when the water reached the usually dry, untouched sand...just subtle, arching lines, replaced a few minutes later by a stronger wave, forming a different but just as subtle crease in the sand.

And it made me miss those people in my life that existed close enough to reach that place of vulnerability within me, but who stayed only long enough to form a soft crease...to be replaced by the next person to come along.

Hypocrite

Hypocrisy is the reflection of self-criticism and absence of self-discipline.

Investments

I've been thinking about thinking.

And the conflict between decisions and memories.

Are we more than our decisions?

Are we more than our memories?

Surely there can not be decisions without memories.

But surely there can be memories without decisions?

What's left once we can no longer make memories…

Can we still make decisions?

And once our bodies have left, surely our memory will remain.

But not the memories we made, only a memory of memories collected.

However, once our bodies have left, our decisions will remain.

Decisions collected and played out over time, generation to generation.

Where should we invest more?

Into the decisions or memories?

Memories that will live and die with us.

Decisions that will ripple long after we are gone.

I've been thinking about thinking.

And the relationship between decisions and memories.

Resentment

It's as if you've collected these pieces and formed an inaccurate picture of me. I can see that you're conflicted, that your resentment shadows your experience. Regardless. I will shine.

Sobriety

I have found alcohol's promises to be as empty as the bottle it comes in. Don't get stuck at the bottom.

Innocence

I would spend time with my niece every Thursday afternoon and when it was hot enough, we'd retreat to the pool. One Thursday, we had the pool all to ourselves so I unabashedly committed to the game we were playing.

I let her hang on to me as I'd swim to various locations within the pool, guided by her direction. My mind welcomed the imaginative landscape that we created to navigate together.

"All aboard! The water train will soon be departing! You'll need to have your ticket ready!" I shouted.

..."I don't have a ticket"

"Grab a leaf" I whispered.

...

"Alright lady Ellie, where are we headed?" I asked.

..."The Shallow Sea...? Like the shallow end of the pool"

"Alrighty! Chugga chugga choo chooo. You need to be prepared to recite the secret password before ascending the stairs and passing through the gate" I explained.

...

"As in you gotta guess the password before climbing the steps" I whispered.

..."*Ah! Umm....magic password!*"

I let her fiddle about on secret adventures to discover hidden treasure, hunt unicorns, and socialize with other princesses.

"*I'm ready for the next stop and I have a leaf-I mean ticket ready for you this time. I want to go to Castle Cove!*"

"You may encounter the Nice Dragon in this land. If he likes you, he'll invite you for tea. But beware invisible trolls! You'll know they're near by being splashed"

She was occupied by the pursuit of ingredients for a magic spell as the worries of adult life started to creep back in and my mind wandered to the land of bills, career choices, and what to eat for dinner.

"*Water train! I need to go somewhere else!*"

"I'm afraid the water train is out of commission for the rest of the day"

..."*What?*"

"The water train is broken"

"*Broken how?*"

"Well I guess there's a part not working right and it needs replaced"

"*Okay let's get someone to fix it! How long has it been broken?*"

"For a long time without knowing it, which is why fixing it will take extra work."

At that point I looked into her big brown eyes full of concern and confusion and saw into the complete innocence, wonder, and hope of a child, and knew she was trying to decipher the shattered, broken, and stained windows of my adult blue eyes and that's when they shattered a little more, knowing that clear, visible window into her safe world would eventually mirror the damaged window of mine.

Mirrors

When I meet or interact with another person, I can't help but to see and appreciate the characteristics in them that remind me of the ones I love.

See, I love a handful of people, but those people are vastly different in personality, opinions, lifestyles...it's hard to escape the traces of them evident in others.

These reflections remind me of the infinite characteristics a single person can possess; how it is inevitable that some of those will overlap with the characteristics and mannerisms of those around them.

It also makes me think about how truly difficult it is to love someone unconditionally.

I believe that God loves us unconditionally, and that he has the advantage of knowing us fully-- down to the number of hairs on our head.

That's the disadvantage for us...not being able to ever fully know someone leaves you vulnerable to their infinite intricacies.

If you can't completely know someone, there might always be something there, waiting to break your heart.

But I guess that's the risk of true unconditional love and the commitment of marriage...saying "I do" to whatever changes and surprises you might discover in yourself and them along the way.

And that's the other thing! People change.

People are supposed to change. Everyone knows that the fastest way from point A to point B is a straight line, but of course life doesn't happen in neat, straight lines.

An individual's relationship with love, loss, adventure, curiosity constantly fluctuates, creating a crazy roller coaster of squiggly lines representing one's life.

So the chances of your line intersecting with another individual's line is nearly impossible...not to mention the fluctuation of their line, leaving you vulnerable to the risk of steadily growing apart from one another or just barely missing each other.

So yeah...the idea of true, unconditional love is kind of exhausting, which is why recognizing those glimmers of semblance offer respite and comfort. How can I not gravitate towards and appreciate those warped reflections of the ones closest to me?

And if I look with enough grace and self-love...I can even see reflections of myself.

Dilemma

Sometimes I wonder what came first: thoughts or feelings?
Chicken or the egg?
The human condition is to feel.
If I had to imagine, feelings directed thoughts:
I feel hungry: how can I find sustenance?
Hunt and gather.
I feel cold: how can I create warmth?
Fire.
I feel sad: how can I feel better?
Tears.
So maybe the human dilemma is not to feel, but learning to differentiate unhealthy emotional responses from healthy coping mechanisms.

Affirmation

Partners love to ask their significant other that trivial yet infuriating little question "would you still love me if I was a worm?"

But I think the intention of the question is overlooked and the implication of needing a thoughtful response is misunderstood.

What they're really asking is "Would you love me despite a change in circumstances? Despite a change in myself? Would you love me in sickness and in health? In poverty and wealth?"

Deeper still, they're asking "Do you love and see me for me, my inner being, my soul?"

A question that carries more significance than assumed.

Expectations

Medical Diagnosis: Mentally Retarded.

Societal Diagnosis: Handicapped. Disabled. Slow.

Familial Truth: Patient, Content, Emotional, Strong, Kind, Capable, Helpful, Consistent, Encouraging, Competitive, Supportive, Intelligent, Playful, Responsible, Independent, Compassionate, Protective, Thoughtful, Loving, Inclusive, Proud, Humorous, Social, Relatable, Optimistic, Peaceful, Simple…

The expectations and presumptions surrounding a diagnosis can make it heavier and more restrictive than it needs to be.

Live your truth.

Unraveling

I believe the full power of memories can only be achieved by shared experiences with others. That's what's so great about inside jokes, a moment shared between people that can be recreated over and over…relationships are strengthened by the memories, moments, and experiences woven together, held tightly by a bond. But when that bond is broken by circumstances, force, or nature, you never really realize the length of thread woven by those memories until the unraveling begins. You'd be surprised at the memories captured in those intricately braided relationships…a poignant, but necessary undoing.

Habits

Instead of looking at the glass half full or half empty, I'm more interested in knowing what the glass of water is being used for.

To water plants?

To water down an alcoholic's whiskey?

Instead of looking at habits as bad or good, I'm more interested in knowing what purpose they serve.

To cope?

To manage?

How is this useful to me?

Inbetween

My absolute favorite kind of weather happens on the days in spring, transitioning to summer. Sunny and low 70s with the sky full of thick and fluffy clouds. Clouds that are shadowed at the bottom so it looks like they're all resting on a glass tabletop...a separation between the heavens and the earth.

Beauty

Art evokes emotion: art uncovers emotion.

Art imitates life.

Life imitates art.

Life evokes art: life uncovers art.

Beauty is in the eye of the beholder.

Sometimes beauty is determined by the artwork, but other times beauty is determined by the feelings…

Beauty is in the eye of the beholder, and life is full of beauty waiting to be uncovered.

Existential

Why is it that when times are good, we anticipate bad?

And when times are bad, we dream of good?

Mountains and Valleys

Ups and Downs

Good and Bad

It's as if we have rejected the homeostatic nature of balance and replaced it with perpetual discontent.

My therapist once asked me if I could allot a percentage of investment of my thoughts and feelings to each of the three categories: Past, Present, and Future.

And I found myself noting that I am either anxiously anticipating the future and attempting to plan for all possible scenarios, or grieving the past and erroneously idolizing events.

A violent fluctuation leaving no room for the present.

Trying to describe my PRESENT state and thoughts proved unfamiliar and uncomfortable.

Good and Bad

Past and Future

Living as instructed by society has neglected space for presence, our thoughts and actions consumed by future choices and past decisions.

Presence is the absence of choices or decisions.

The practice of existing.

The art of living.

Potential

Heartbreak prevention: uncoupling imagined potential from existing probability. Potential is the ultimate click-bait.

Compliments

If you were an inanimate object, you'd be a Rubik's cube.
Irresistibly touchable.
Mysterious.
Bright and fun.
Intellectually stimulating.
And frustrating as f***

Awareness

Sometimes, when the bad of the world overwhelms me, I like to step into that dark space...acquaint myself with the filth, corruption, and brokenness.

I like to hold it in my hands...roll it around...feel the hard, dark, cold penetrate my skin...and at some point I reach a place of familiarity.

The monster under the bed.

The news on tv.

The bad becomes malleable...I'm able to form it into a recognizable shape: fear, shame, guilt.

And at that point, the bad isn't quite as heavy, not as overwhelming...just disappointing.

Disappointing that it is so often overlooked, misunderstood, and unidentified.

I walk out of that space lighter.

Family

The roots of our family tree may be knotted, the leaves may have some holes, the apples might have some worms, and the trunk may have rotted in some places...but I'm proud of our deep roots, colorful leaves, sweet and sour apples, and strong branches.

I endure every winter and celebrate each spring because of my pride in our family tree.

Spirals

I like to imagine the communication within my body: a line from my stomach to my heart to my brain and back down again. Constantly messaging.

"I really want a dessert- no, you're really just sad- so maybe let's eat some fruit to meet in the middle"

However, it isn't a straight line because the body receives and processes stimuli constantly. I would imagine the line of communication more as a spiral: traveling from the top of my head to the tips of my toes, checking in at the major processing units of the stomach, heart, and brain.

If I think about this process of communication, and replay moments of negative internal processing, I can see an extremely tight and constricting spiral. When I recall positive internal processing, it always considers intrinsic and extrinsic factors, creating a wide and open spiral, extending outside of myself.

Furthermore, considering this process is happening within everyone I encounter, I imagine moments when I've clashed with peers. Our spirals wound so tight, interacting against each other like the blades in a shredder. Compared to moments of collaboration when our looping spirals overlapped each other creating gears working together.

Aesthete

I cherish the sweet relief of losing myself in a good song, book, film, or painting. Art has a way of driving my emotions and steering my thoughts for me, I'm able to ride along without the limitation of reaching a destination.

Choices

Environment and circumstances shape our understanding of survival which dictates life choices.

Perspectives

My parents always encouraged me to consider the other side of the story, to imagine looking from someone else's perspective. Being an overachiever, I took that a step further...

I decided to challenge myself to see just how many different sides to a story there could be in any given situation, which began my fascination with and appreciation for gray.

Consider a piece of paper; it has two sides and sits idle on surfaces, pretty hard to flip or turn over unless acted upon by external force.

Perpetuating black and white.

Now a sphere arguably has an infinite amount of sides with maximum mobility, constantly moving, and if it does come to rest, it's on a very small precipice, easily pushed into motion again.

Aimlessly sliding along the color spectrum.

However, a die has six sides with a good bit of mobility, but ultimately comes to rest on one side, displaying a response.

Purposefully exhibiting a shade of gray.

I've come to discover that I have a hard time getting along with pieces of paper, can't stand spheres, and really appreciate those who are willing to roll the dice.

Drafts

Conversation and spoken words are just the rough draft of ideas and opinions.

Confessions

HSV-2.

Three letters, one number, and four syllables.

A sentence.

I have HSV-2.

Three words, one number, and six syllables.

A sentence.

I was assaulted and contracted HSV-2.

Six words, one number, and thirteen syllables.

A sentence.

Dating with HSV-2...

A complicated conversation.

Experienced dating with HSV-2...

A new page.

Meeting someone that makes it past the HSV-2 conversation...

A new chapter.

Being in a relationship with someone who accepts my past, enjoys my presence, and plans for the future...

Indescribable.

Living with HSV-2 and sharing my experiences...

Irreplaceable.

Sometimes you need to re-read a sentence for comprehension, but once you move past that sentence and string together more sentences, that's where you can decide how to apply your knowledge. With application follows mastery.

Start with a sentence, and master your story.

Care

I think the intimacy of fulfilling someone's needs is often overlooked. A lot of times people make assumptions of others' needs based on their conditions rather than their being. Just because someone is "poor" doesn't mean they need money...

Meeting a need for someone communicates care boldly.

Expressing a need from someone communicates vulnerability.

Giving and receiving care communicates trust.

Duality

The most successful people I know have mastered the ability to hold space for logic and emotions simultaneously and equally; a mind that promotes the coexistence of emotions and logic builds the most beneficial reciprocity.

Glow

Love is like a sunburn…

Not just a feeling, but a lesson to be learned.

Experienced in the summers of youth, and exposed to its hard truth.

First encounters are full of ignorant bliss, spent basking in the warmth and radiance of its gentle kiss.

Without caution its exposure can be damaging, causing painful blisters and uncomfortable swelling.

Yet too much caution can result in insignificance, its memory peeled away and passed off as coincidence.

Love is like a sunburn…

Best treated with familiarity and handled with delicacy.

Nurtured with maturity and expressed passionately.

Each exposure now carefully measured, for its purity is meant to be treasured.

With the balance of caution and vulnerability, it can blossom and grow in tranquility.

Now a lesson mastered, it appears a welcome haphazard.

Because in time one will know, when a sunburn will fade into a golden glow.

Simple

It was the third day into the week of house-sitting that she took the time to recall how many interactions with her brother had taken place, and came to the total of three: taking a plate of cookies into his room, checking to see what he wanted to eat for dinner, and asking him to bring the mail in. She needed to do better. He deserved better.

She contemplated options for things to do as she stared at his closed bedroom door and began unpacking the box in her brain storing all things Max. Max was simple: he liked his truck and anything patriotic, he hated conflict, and he did not eat cheese. She was younger than him by eight years, but in ways older than him. Max had "special needs" according to society, and "mentally disabled" according to doctors. To her, he was just Max: her older brother who always wanted to help, loved to laugh, and show off his pictures that captured some of his favorite memories.

She decided a walk would be good, it would at least get him out of his room. As she approached his bedroom door, she prepared to cross the threshold into his world and reached into that place of patience and kindness. She knocked before entering and found him in his usual spot: sitting in his chair, legs folded beneath him, elbow propped on the armrest as he watched whatever episode of Walker, Texas Ranger was on. He looked to her with eyebrows raised, awaiting the reason for disruption.

"I was thinking about going for a walk down the street, want to come" she posed the question casually to ease any perceived pressure for one answer over the other. No response, meaning probably not. "I was thinking we could take the dog for a walk because she needs exercise and the weather is nice outside" she threw in two factors for leverage: the dog whom he loved and the weather which he always checked. Max decided "let me put my shoes on first, you might need a jacket because it's cold outside". Success.

They walked at a leisurely pace as she prompted conversation with specific questions about his truck and what he's watched on tv lately, which were received with brief responses. They continued in comfortable silence for a while until her mind drifted to her current life situation and used the opportunity to process externally. She enjoyed his company in these moments because she didn't have to offer detailed explanations, context, or analysis to him, she could simply talk without being self-conscious. Max expressed interest through his laughs and "mhmm"s.

When she felt like she covered the topics at the forefront of her mind, she noticed the sky getting darker and suggested they make their way back home. On the way back, she reviewed her freshly processed thoughts which led to new information and revelations to breakdown. Max seemed to notice the shift and made a comment on the weather, and she was grateful for his understanding. As night fell and they made it back to the driveway, she looked up at the sky and the emerging stars. She asked Max "I've always wanted to learn the constellations and be able to point them out, do you know any of the constellations up there? I know I can find Orion's belt and sometimes one of the dippers, but it's frustrating trying to piece them all together sometimes". Max studied the sky with her, but turned to face her with bright green eyes as he said "all I see are stars".

Maternal

Push through the discomfort. Life is born through discomfort.

Reverence

If God exists, and I believe he does, then I would imagine his characteristics to resemble the full and perfect form of his creation and more...

Standing mightily above us, surpassing the mountains' ridge lines, and exceeding the abundant sky.

Yet gently sloping down to earth, providing hills and valleys for us to traverse, so that we may know ourselves and inherently him more.

As infinite as the blades of grass or stars and ever active as the swirling wind.

As refreshing as streams of water and as powerful as thunderstorms.

Winter, Spring, Summer, and Fall.

Beginning and end.

Maker of heaven and earth.

And if we are part of his creation, do we not resemble the creator and possess a fragment of his characteristics?

If we simultaneously looked upward and inward, would we be surprised by the abundance of complexity, power, and compassion we contain?

Freckles

I'd like to imagine each freckle as a permanent commemoration of summer experiences:

Learning to ride a bike in Florida

A summer fling in Montana

Kayaking in Ireland

Family reunions in Tennessee and Mississippi

Leaving a cruise ship with a new long-distance friend

Bachelorette trips in South Carolina

Camping in Arkansas

Tiny melanin tattoos creating a constellation of sleepless nights and warm memories.

I used to hope as a child that I would collect more and more freckles until they merged together forming one golden tan...a perpetual summer.

It's not that I hated my pale skin…just that I hated winters. Winter proved to be a tumultuous time every year from deaths, breakups, assaults, and loneliness…experiences that penetrated deeper than the sun could ever reach. I hated feeling like my skin exposed the inner emptiness and exhaustion consuming my insides. I hated being able to trace my veins as if the transparency extended deeper into my being, displaying my hurts and hang-ups for all to see.

It wasn't until I experienced summer after summer, winter after winter, that I realized the changing of the seasons, the transition, was where the beauty was found. The intersection of good and bad.

Contrast.

Enough

She broke herself into pieces, not seeing the beautiful mosaic her pieces created until looking at herself through his eyes.

Sacrifice

Mom, I used to think you talked the sun into rising every morning. Awakened by the smell of syrup and bacon, I remember checking my clock and calculating that I had ten minutes before my alarm sounded- just enough time for me to scurry from my bunk bed, turn my alarm off, and climb back into bed to play possum. Ten minutes later, you walked into my room singing *Give God the Glory* and reached up to scratch my head until I opened my eyes. Those mornings made me believe in gentleness, trust in kindness, and delight in hope.

Dad, I used to think you hung the moon each evening, and set the stars twinkling. I remember wearing my favorite set of pajamas as I huddled on the living room couch to watch my blockbuster movie, and not being the least bit sleepy as the credits rolled. Contemplating the stillness of the house, I picked up the remote and started the movie all over again just to fall asleep on the couch so you could carry me to bed. Those evenings made me believe in consistency, trust in strength, and delight in mystery.

Mom, I know you talked yourself into rising every morning just to cook a warm breakfast for our family, even though you'd be the last one to sit and eat. I know you were awake an hour earlier than me to make sure my school clothes were washed and dry for the day. I also know you knew I was only pretending to be asleep. I will forever be grateful for your gentleness, kindness, and teaching me to live with hope.

Dad, I know you came home exhausted from work, just to meet the ongoing needs of our family. I know you stayed awake late at night, planning out the days ahead. I know your joints creaked and complained as you scooped me off of the couch, carried me to my room, and placed me in my bed. I also know you knew I fell asleep on the couch on purpose. I will forever be grateful for your consistency, strength, and quiet servitude.

Mom and dad, thank you for your unconditional love and sacrifices.

Community

Compassion is the difference between what you see and who you see.

Heartbroken

Loving and losing you is different from having loved and lost anyone else.

I've experienced heartbreak, but losing you is being heartbroken.

Verb: heartbreak- an exploitation.

Heartbreak was frantic and desperate, the all-consuming knowledge that *they* didn't love *me*.

Noun: heartbroken- a state of being.

Heartbroken is calm and peaceful, sure of the fact that *I* love *you*...regardless of reciprocation.

Unconditional.

Unapologetic.

Unwavering.

Purpose

The sound of the wind grew louder as it rushed through the tall pine trees, carrying with it a sense of urgency. She hastened her steps in case the wind brought with it the impending rain drops weighing down the clouds, but stopped abruptly to watch the trees swaying.

As she looked up into the high branches, she pitied the pine trees...their restless movement agitated by the relentless wind, yet rooted firmly in their position. She was overwhelmed by gratitude for the legs beneath her and the freedom of choice: to run from the incoming storm, to walk into it head on, or to stand in place as the wind swirled around her.

As she stood there in the middle of the narrow road nestled in her small Louisiana neighborhood, she focused her gaze beyond the pine branches and into the murky clouds, imagining what was beyond...

With her face turned up towards the sky, she felt a raindrop land in the corner of her eye and trace a path along her nose and drip off of her chin landing on the ground. Just the first of many drops.

With one foot in front of the other, she passed the towering pines as her mind painted fields of the most colorful wildflowers.

www.ingramcontent.com/pod-product-compliance
Lightning Source LLC
LaVergne TN
LVHW012032060526
838201LV00061B/4564